Are You a Roundhead or a Cavalier?

Contents

Written by Juliet Kerrigan

Illustrated by Max Marin

Collins

Whose side are you on?

I'm Lady Margaret. My husband and I support Charles Stuart, who became king in 1625. We're Royalists, and our nickname Cavalier means "horseman". You can recognise us by our longer hair, hats with feathers, lace collars and riding boots with spurs. But it's not just how you look, it's what you believe that's important.

I'm Robert Brown. My wife and I support **parliament**. Our nickname Roundhead comes from the shape of our soldiers' helmets, or maybe it's our men's short haircuts. We wear plain clothes, and we have strong views about how the country should be ruled.

FAKE NEWS

Roundheads don't all wear black clothes; black dye is expensive.

Spotlight on Charles I

The king is a serious-minded man, devoted to his wife Henrietta Maria and their children. He rules by divine right, which means he gets his authority from God, as his father did. He makes the laws, demands taxes, chooses his advisers and decides how to run the country. His Majesty is the head of the Church of England.

Spotlight on parliament

The king isn't above the law! He should respect the opinions of the 600 members of the House of Commons.
They represent the views of people who matter – landowners.
The king claims he's not rich, but if he wants more money, he needs parliament to agree.

FAKE NEWS

It might sound like fake news, but there really was an earthquake at Charles I's coronation.

Money problems

The king may own palaces like Whitehall in London, land all over the country and fabulous collections of paintings and jewels, but he needs money if he's going to rule England, Wales, Scotland and Ireland. If he has to fight a war against France or crush a rebellion, he'll need soldiers, warships, cannons and gunpowder.

In 1626, the king decided to raise money by introducing a new tax. Parliament didn't agree to this! Anyone who didn't pay up was sent to prison without trial. Members of Parliament (MPs) also disliked the king's adviser, the Duke of Buckingham. When they drew up a list of complaints, Charles closed parliament down for six months. When it met again, there were even more complaints about the king's behaviour.

FAKE NEWS

The Cavaliers call Buckingham a great man, but he's a disaster as a commander.

Time out

What was the king to do? The Duke of Buckingham was murdered in 1628 – stabbed by an angry army officer – and parliament was still not willing to grant **lawful** taxes or agree to the changes His Majesty wanted in the way the church was run. In March 1629, the king had to **dissolve** a defiant parliament and arrest nine MPs. That showed them who really rules.

Some of the nine MPs were imprisoned in the Tower of London.

Parliament was shut down for 11 years! That's wrong – there's no one to speak on behalf of the people. How would you feel about that? The king was so short of money, he searched through old records to find other ways of taxing his people. What did he come up with? Ship money! This was money raised from taxes for building ships used to defend England from enemies. It was meant to be for emergencies, not taken from people time and again.

Name: John Hampden

Occupation: Member of Parliament

Crime: refused to pay ship money

War?

In 1637, when the king introduced some changes to the church in Scotland, there was a riot – how **unseemly**! The English army went to sort the trouble out and soon made peace, but it didn't last, and the Scots invaded England. And I hear the Irish are in revolt because they don't like their English landlords. The king really needs those taxes for defence – they're his right.

People in Scotland threw chairs and stools!

It's 1640. The king is so poor, he's **recalled** parliament and asked for money. Many people in England didn't support sending an army to Scotland – not even the army itself. There's unrest everywhere. I've heard the words "Cavalier" and "Roundhead" used as insults.

Cavaliers (left) and Roundheads (right) being rude to each other

FAKE NEWS

Don't let anyone tell you that the king arrested another five MPs in January 1642. He tried to, but they escaped! One of them was John Hampden.

Weapons check

The king planned to send an army to Ireland, but parliament wanted to be in control of it, and the king couldn't allow that. His Majesty sent messages to all areas of England asking for soldiers.

The king commands 15 foot regiments, armed with swords, muskets and pikes up to five metres long, eight **cavalry** regiments and some **dragoons**.

Parliament has also asked for soldiers, so now's the moment for people to choose. People in London, the south-east and east are responding well. These are the richer, more **populated** areas. I hear some families are split. The MP Sir Edmund Verney supports the king, but his son Ralph supports us.

Live report: Battle of Edgehill

It's 23rd October 1642 and the king has gathered an army of 14,000 men at Edgehill. The king, riding a magnificent horse, is wearing a steel cap covered in velvet. His nephew, Prince Rupert, commands four cavalry regiments and has charged through the Roundhead forces. After three hours, the king is **victorious**.

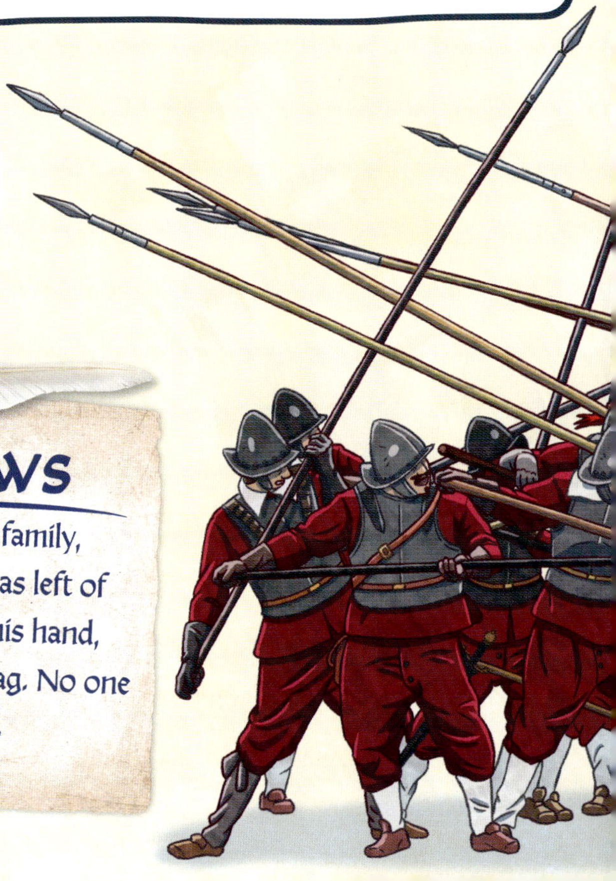

FAKE NEWS

According to the Verney family, after the battle, all that was left of Sir Edmund Verney was his hand, still clutching the royal flag. No one knows if it's actually true.

We have a similar number of men, led by the Earl of Essex. He gave the signal to fire at 3 o'clock in the afternoon. Like the Cavaliers, the soldiers have little experience of battle, but our officers are well trained. Prince Rupert is so keen to chase away our cavalry that he's ridden right off the battlefield! As night falls, there are over 1,000 dead. Don't believe the Cavalier fake news! We haven't lost. The king could have marched to London if he'd been smarter. Now he's made Oxford his capital.

Spotlight on Prince Rupert

Prince Rupert is the king's not-so-secret weapon. He's been a soldier in Europe since he was 18 and knows what he's doing. He's an example to all the king's supporters.

All Prince Rupert's interested in is burning towns and seizing **loot**. He's known as the "Robber Prince". It's said that his white poodle, Boy, who goes into battle with him, has special powers.

FAKE NEWS

Some say Boy can catch bullets in his teeth, but no one has ever seen him do it.

Civil War spies

We need to know what's going on behind the scenes. Women can be useful spies because people think they're too **virtuous** to do such dastardly work! They're called "intelligencers". I have my doubts about Lady Percy. She's close to the queen but whose side is she really on? Someone warned those five MPs in 1642 that the king was going to arrest them. Is she a double agent?

Lady Percy. Spy.
Double agent?

We too need information. I hear our spies are given numbers or false names. They can make invisible ink with lemon or artichoke juice. The clever part is to write alternate lines in ordinary ink – a blank page in a letter would look suspicious. If you heat the paper, the hidden message appears. Even more clever is to write in code, folding the paper so craftily you can tell if the enemy has opened it first.

Spotlight on Oliver Cromwell

Who is this **upstart** Cromwell? I hear he only spent one year at the University of Cambridge and has been an MP since 1628. He's always been a troublemaker; when the king ordered the Cambridge colleges to send him all the silver they owned, Cromwell and some volunteers blocked the road and took the silver back.

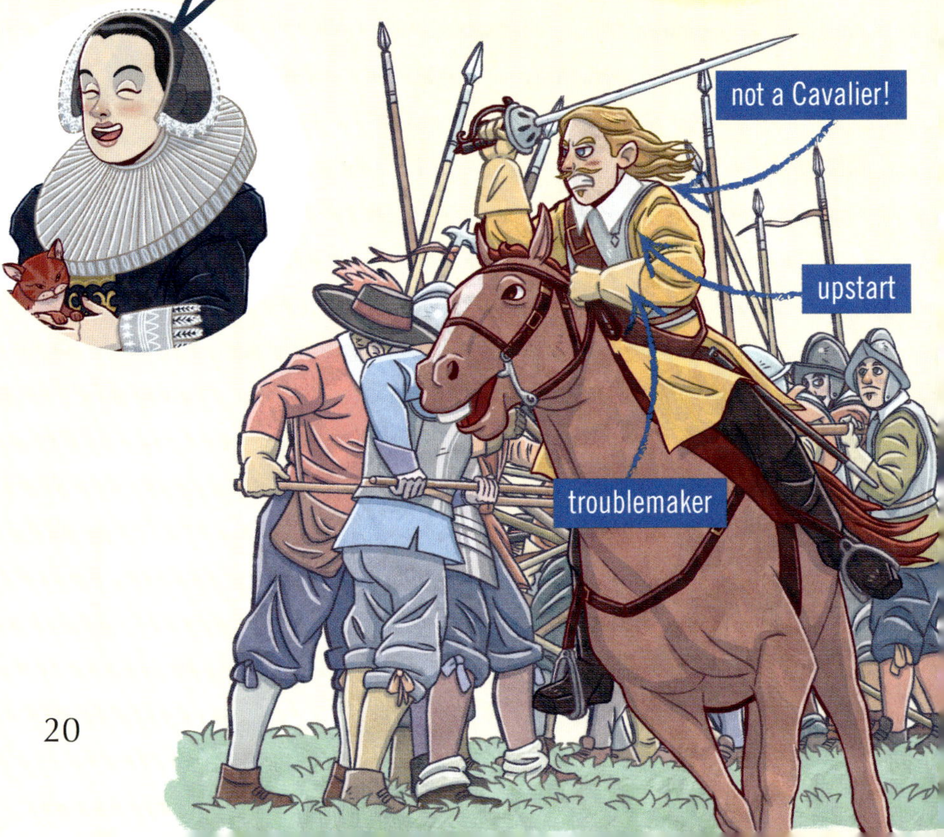

Oliver Cromwell has always supported parliament. He comes from a farming family and fought at Edgehill. He's proved himself a worthy soldier and he's already taken the ports of Lowestoft and King's Lynn for parliament. He thinks soldiers should believe in the cause they're fighting for.

Spotlight on women and the war effort

In 1643, news arrived that Lady Mary Bankes refused to surrender Corfe Castle despite being **besieged** by over 500 Roundheads. She, her daughters and servants threw stones and hot embers over the battlements to stop the soldiers climbing the walls. The soldiers ran off and Corfe survived to see another day.

Roundhead women have been playing their part, too. Lady Brilliana Harley defended Brampton Bryan Castle from a Royalist army while her husband was in London. In 1643, Royalists burnt the nearby village, stole her cattle and sheep and bombarded the castle with cannons, fired from the church roof. Brilliana held out for nearly a year.

Lady Brilliana Harley

Live report: Battle of Marston Moor

It's 2nd July 1644, and we Cavaliers are outnumbered at Marston Moor by a hotch-potch of Scots and parliament's forces. Prince Rupert is in command of the cavalry and at first he has the upper hand, despite being caught by surprise.

FAKE NEWS

Did Jane Ingleby dress as a man and fight for the king at Marston Moor? Did she hold Cromwell at gunpoint when he turned up at her home, Ripley Castle, allowing her brother to escape? No one knows for sure!

Cromwell's **Ironsides** have triumphed! There are 4,000 Royalists dead. After two hours, the Cavaliers have retreated to York but they won't last long there. Prince Rupert has been spotted hiding in a bean field and his dog has gone missing.

Where's Rupert?

BATTLE SCORE 2: Roundhead victory

Spotlight on the New Model Army

the army discussing plans

The army is going to be reorganised under Sir Thomas Fairfax. We hope to have 14,400 **infantry** in red uniform. Oliver Cromwell will be second-in-command and in charge of 6,600 cavalry. Officers will be promoted on merit, not because they come from an important family.

Live report: Battle of Naseby

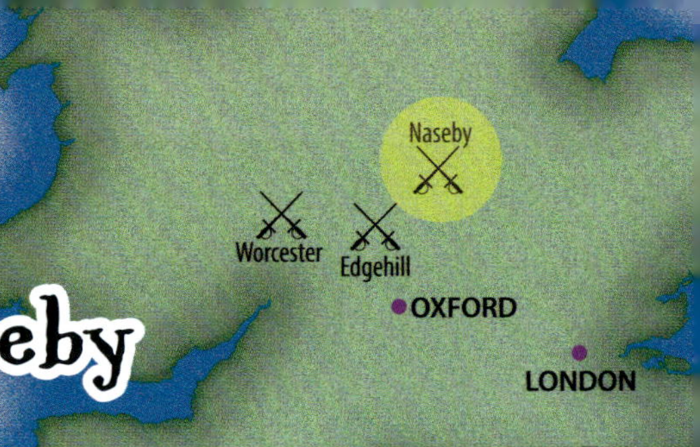

We Cavaliers were doing so well in the Midlands and north-west but now, on 14th June 1645, we're facing the enemy at Naseby. Despite being outnumbered, Prince Rupert's cavalry broke through the Roundheads. Then he made the same mistake as before, riding off the battlefield to attack the **baggage train** and returning too late.

FAKE NEWS

Some say the king charged into battle but this might not be true. If you were giving orders, would it be better to ride into battle or stay behind your troops?

The New Model Army, led by Fairfax and Cromwell, proved itself today. The Royalist army is defeated, and we have their **artillery** and supplies. This is the end for them – they can't defend Bristol and Oxford for long. Oliver wrote to parliament: "Honest men served you faithfully."

This painting of Oliver Cromwell, on horseback at the Battle of Naseby, was painted over 200 years later. This is how the Victorians pictured the event.

What next for the king?

The king escaped from Oxford in 1646 and he's now with the Scots at Southwell. Our enemies are so divided among themselves, I'm sure he can get back to where he rightfully belongs. Prince Rupert believes the king should **negotiate** with the Roundheads.

the tavern, called the King's Head, where Charles spent what was to become his last night of freedom

I foresee problems. The Scots and parliament have different ideas from the army about what should happen next. The army won the war and the soldiers' ideas should be listened to. Many soldiers, including Oliver Cromwell, are **tolerant**. They don't accept the law saying everyone must go to church on Sunday.

This woodcut shows the world turned upside down, which is how some people felt about what was happening.

Live report: Battle of Preston

In January 1647, the Scots handed the king over to parliament. The Scots wanted £400,000 for him but I hear parliament paid £100,000.

The news is that some loyal Scots have invaded England to rescue the king and now, on 17th August 1648, they're facing the New Model Army at Preston.

£100,000 in coins would have been very heavy and awkward to transport. How would you do it?

Things have been happening fast! In June 1647, a lowly officer with 500 soldiers seized the king at Holdenby House in Northamptonshire. He was placed under house arrest at Hampton Court but in November 1647 he escaped.

It's now 1648 and the Scots haven't a hope here at Preston – Cromwell's army triumphs again.

Captured in the castle

News has it the king hoped to sail to France but ended up on the Isle of Wight. He's in touch with both the queen and the Scots and wants to escape from Carisbrook Castle where he's being "looked after" by the Roundhead governor. One attempt to escape failed because the king got stuck in a window. Two saws and some acid were smuggled in to cut the window bars, but the governor found out.

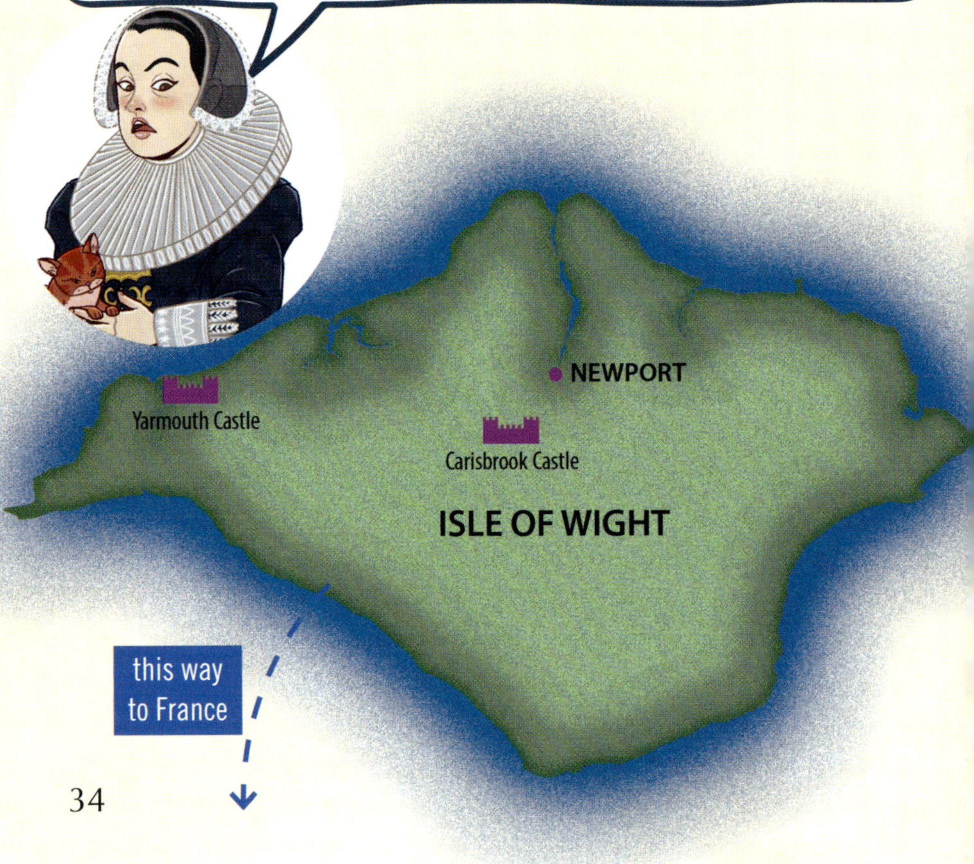

Parliament has sent men to the Isle of Wight to negotiate with the king, but the army is angry about this. Members of the army called him "Charles Stuart, that man of blood" and they marched into London. Over 200 MPs who support the king have been thrown out of parliament. About 100 MPs chose to stay away. Nothing stands in the way of the army putting Charles on trial.

Trial and execution

The army had no choice. On 20th January 1649, Charles was tried in Westminster Hall, London, and accused of waging war on his own subjects – that's treason! The king said he didn't recognise the court and kept his hat on as a sign of disrespect. He's been found guilty of plotting in secret with the Scots, so he's untrustworthy too. His death warrant was signed by 59 commissioners.

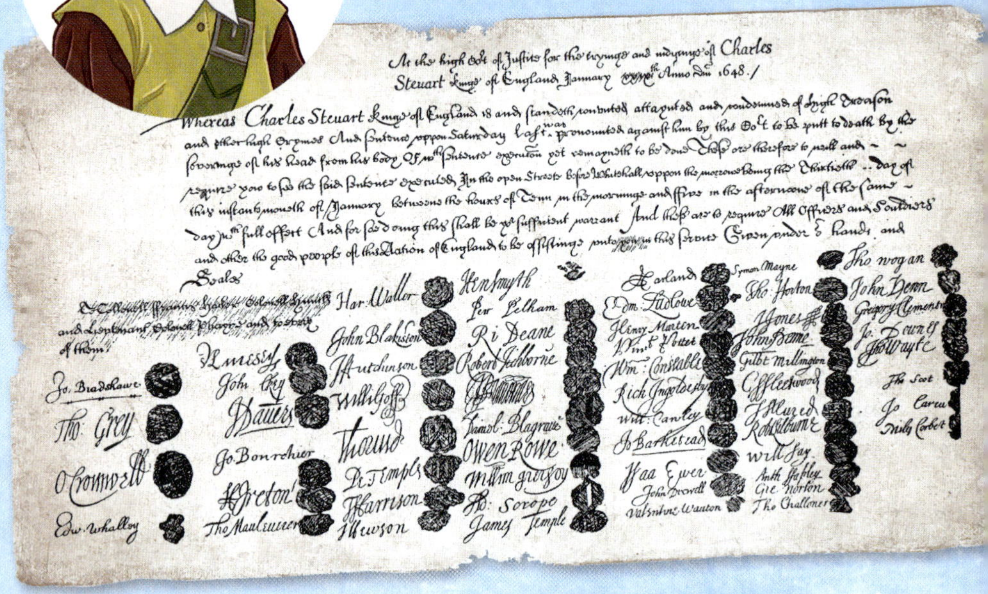

At the high Court of Justice for the tryinge and judginge of Charles Steuart Kinge of England January xxix Anno Dni 1648.

Whereas Charles Steuart Kinge of England is and standeth convicted attaynted and condemned of High Treason and other high Crymes And sentence uppon Saturday last was pronounced against him by this Court to be putt to death by the severinge of his head from his body Of wch sentence execucon yet remayneth to be done These are therefore to will and require you to see the said sentence executed In the open Streete before Whitehall uppon the morrowe being the Thirtieth day of this instante moneth of January betweene the houres of Tenn in the morninge and Five in the afternoone of the same day wth full effect And for soe doing this shall be yor sufficient warrant And these are to require All Officers and Souldiers and other the good people of this Nation of England to be assistinge unto you in this service Given under our hands and Seales.

Can you find Cromwell's signature?

Horrifying scenes were witnessed at Whitehall, London, on 30th January 1649. The king was led in front of the Banqueting House and, after giving a noble and courageous speech, he was executed. At least the executioner was skilful – it only took one blow of his axe. A witness reported there "was such a groan by the thousands then present".

FAKE NEWS

Charles wore two shirts so no one would think he was shivering from fear. Fake or not?

The Commonwealth

The monarchy has been **abolished** and England is now a **republic**. Freedom to worship has been given to most Christian groups. There are some strange new ideas around. Some think the end of the world will come, while a group called the Levellers have suggested everyone should have the vote – even women!

Oliver Cromwell shown cutting down an oak tree, which represents the monarchy

The king has quietly been buried at Windsor. A book he is said to have written, explaining all these events, has become a bestseller. Far from being a murderer, he died for his beliefs. As for these new-fangled ideas – they won't last!

This illustration was at the front of the king's book.

More war

We Cavaliers haven't given up hope. Some of the republic's plans aren't popular. There were riots when Christmas was abolished! Royalist **exiles** in Europe are plotting. I've heard of a secretive group called the Sealed Knot who want to restore the monarchy. Cromwell's spymaster, John Thurloe, is watching them.

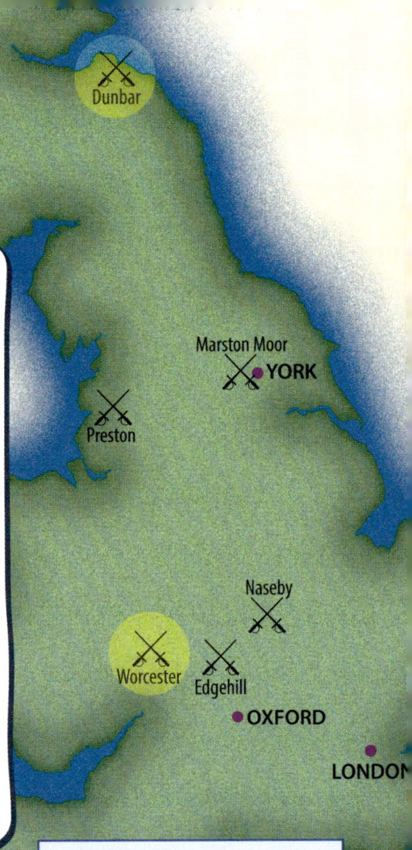

enemy of the Cavaliers, John Thurloe

Cromwell hasn't been able to step back from warfare – he wants to crush those Irish rebels and the Scots who back Charles I's son, who's also called Charles. On 3rd September 1650, Cromwell had a famous victory at Dunbar. A year later, when the Scots invaded again, young Charles was with them. But Cromwell defeated them at Worcester.

BATTLE SCORE 5 and 6: Roundhead victories

FAKE NEWS

Young Charles hid in an oak tree after the battle at Worcester. This might be true … or it might not.

The Restoration, 1660

Oliver Cromwell was a good man, not a **tyrant**. He accepted the title Lord Protector but turned down being king. He's dead now but he didn't make any plans about what would happen after his death, and his son Richard's not up to the task.

It's time for us to celebrate! General George Monck has marched into England. He used to support Cromwell, but he's not happy with the New Model Army and the way it's ruling England. There are new MPs in parliament, and they're Royalists. King Charles I's son has been invited back from Europe. He'll be crowned King Charles II. Will you be out rejoicing?

The republic lasted 11 years, but now the Stuarts are back. Will their power last ...?
You've heard it from both sides, so would you have been a Roundhead or a Cavalier?

Glossary

abolished got rid of

artillery weapons like cannon

baggage train carts carrying army supplies

besieged surrounded a town or castle with soldiers to capture it

cavalry soldiers who fight on horseback

dissolve close down parliament and order new elections of MPs

dragoons soldiers who ride to the battlefield, then dismount to fight

exiles people living away from where they come from, usually unwillingly

infantry foot soldiers

Ironsides Cromwell and his soldiers, so called for their hardiness in battle

lawful according to the rules

loot valuables, which could be gold or silver or chickens!

negotiate reach a decision by discussion

parliament House of Lords (nobles) and House of Commons (elected MPs)

populated having people living there

recalled brought back

republic country without a monarch, with power held by the people

tolerant willing to accept other people's views and beliefs

tyrant cruel ruler

unseemly impolite

upstart a person behaving as though they're better than they are

victorious have won

virtuous someone with good moral qualities and behaviour

Index

Who said what?

Who is a Roundhead and who is a Cavalier?

Women are good at defending castles.

The king can do whatever he wants.

Members of Parliament should have more say.

The people should have more say.

Banish Christmas!

We need money to defend England!

Parliament is in charge of the money.
Women make excellent spies!
Buckingham is a good commander!
Prince Rupert is a robber!
I believe in divine right.
We need a republic!

Ideas for reading

Gill Matthews
Primary Literacy Consultant

Reading objectives:

- check that the text makes sense to them, discuss their understanding and explaining the meaning of words in context
- ask questions to improve their understanding of a text
- identify main ideas drawn from more than one paragraph and summarising these
- retrieve and record information from non-fiction

Spoken language objectives:

- ask relevant questions to extend their understanding and knowledge
- use relevant strategies to build their vocabulary
- articulate and justify answers, arguments and opinions

Curriculum links: History: a study of an aspect or theme in British history that extends pupils' chronological knowledge beyond 1066

Interest words: devoted, authority, respect, represent, claims

Build a context for reading

- Ask children to look closely at the front cover of the book. Discuss what clues there are about the content of the book. Explore their knowledge and understanding of Roundheads and Cavaliers.
- Read the back-cover blurb. Ask the children what they think they will find out from the book. Explore any words and phrases that are unfamiliar to the children and support them in working out their meaning.
- Point out that this is an information book. Ask what features the children expect to find in the book.
- Ask children to turn to the contents page. Establish the purpose of a contents and how it is organised.
- Ask children to use the contents to find the chapter *Whose side are you on?*